The Sayings of Bernard Shaw

The Sayings of

BERNARD
SHAW

edited by
Joseph Spence

Duckworth

This impression 2002
First published in 1993 by
Gerald Duckworth & Co. Ltd.
61 Frith Street, London W1D 3JL
Tel: 020 7434 4242
Fax: 020 7434 4420
inquiries@duckworth-publishers.co.uk
www.ducknet.co.uk

A catalogue record for this book is available
from the British Library

ISBN 0 7156 2491 1

Printed in Great Britain by
Antony Rowe Ltd, Eastbourne

Contents

For Angela,

with love

Introduction

Although he asserted that there was no such thing as an Irish race (all races being mongrel races), Shaw added that there was, however, an Irish climate which marked a man indelibly. He acknowledged openly how deeply his own particular Irishness affected his development. It fuelled that ambition which drove him to become one of the most popular and controversial literary figures of the twentieth century. It influenced his thinking on literature, politics and morality to a greater extent than any other factor. To understand him, therefore, it is necessary to see him in his Irish context.

George Bernard Shaw was born in a small house on Upper Synge Street, Dublin, in late July 1856. He was the third child of a shabby-genteel, drunken father and his long-suffering wife, whose one consolation was her association with a local celebrity, the musician George Vandeleur Lee. Thus Shaw grew up in that *demi-monde* Dublin, the façade of which, at least, has been vividly described in the opening paragraph of Somerville and Ross's *The Real Charlotte* (1895). The north side of Dublin is the epitome 'of all that is hot, arid, and empty', a world of 'stifling squares' and tall brick houses 'browbeating each other in gloomy respectability'. It is said that few towns are duller out of season than Dublin, but that 'the dullness of its north side neither waxes nor wanes; it is immutable, unchangeable, fixed as the stars'. This is how Shaw saw it and he confided to Ellen Terry that he had had a depressing childhood, 'rich only in dreams, frightful and loveless in realities'.

Shaw's parents boasted ancestors of some wealth and personal distinction, but he realised early in life that his social standing was uncertain. He had been born into an insecure Protestant merchant class which sustained its self-respect by believing that every Protestant, whatever his or her present lot, was superior to every Catholic.

'Irish Protestantism was not then a religion', Shaw
reflected, 'it was a side in political faction, a class
prejudice, a conviction that Roman Catholics are socially
inferior persons who will go to Hell when they die and
leave Heaven in the exclusive possession of Protestant
ladies and gentlemen.'

For all this posturing, however, the poorer Protestants
not only lacked the social confidence of the Protestant
Ascendancy, they also lacked the sense of community of
the Catholics. Their society, such as it was, was brittle,
artificial and stultifying. It was also prudish, and the
puritanical element in Shaw's character can be traced to
his envy of those Dublin 'jackeens' – like those he
recognized in Joyce's *Ulysses* – who seemed free from
lasting guilt about sex.

With his head full of Shakespeare and Dickens, and
the music of Mozart and Wagner, Shaw left Dublin in
1876, at the age of twenty. Living principally for art,
music and literature, he found a haven in London in the
British Museum. Its library was to be Shaw's university.
He was almost completely self-taught and his writings
are evidently the work of a man who, in his formative
years, never had his opinions challenged. Not that the
young Shaw was over-confident, however, and in his
early years in London, he was like one of the displaced
persons of MacNeice's 'The British Museum Reading
Room'. Shaw could have remained one of the library's
'stooping haunted readers', a British Museum 'refugee',
had it not been for William Archer, the drama critic who
set him on the road to becoming a playwright. Archer
had sought an introduction to Shaw because he was
intrigued to meet a man whom he had seen poring over
a French translation of *Das Kapital* and the score of
Tristan and Isolde – at the same time. A strong brew of
Marx and Wagner was the sort of heady mixture Shaw
was to offer his readers and playgoers for the next sixty
years.

Emerging from the half-life of the Museum, Shaw
found that success, first as a critic and then as a
playwright (with a New York production of *The Devil's
Disciple* in 1897), gave him the confidence to adopt in

public the persona of Mephistopheles, to whom he had likened himself since his youth. Shaw remained a Mephistophelian taunter of canting individuals and establishments for the rest of his ninety-four years, during which time he raised social criticism to the level of an art form.

Shaw may have denied that race had any meaning, but the success of his social criticism owed a great deal to the fact that he was an Irishman in England. He always enjoyed being the outspoken Irish boy wonder (albeit a distinctly middle-aged prodigy) who saw exactly what was wrong with the Empire's new clothes. He was among the most effective of that succession of Irish observers of English life who had played such an important part in the progress of English literature and, especially, English drama since the eighteenth century. Harsher than Goldsmith, wittier than Burke or Yeats and more demanding than Sheridan, Farquhar or Congreve, Shaw came close to Wilde in his aphoristic skill and closest to Swift in the boldness of his satirical prose (although he lacked that 'savage indignation' which crowns Swift's greatness). All these Anglo-Irishmen 'cast a cold eye' on their English neighbour, exposing the hypocrisy, artifice and absurdity of his world. What enabled them to portray English society with such accuracy was the fact that they were both insiders and outsiders: they were able to assimilate easily once in London, but, by birth and breeding, they were from a different tradition.

Shaw saw his Irishness as excluding him from being in any sense English (the idea of Anglo-Irishness was not one he ever discussed). 'I am not myself an Englishman but an Irishman,' he said, 'and all my national prejudice is anti-English.' There was a coda to this statement, however: 'But one of the first things Socialism taught me was that national prejudices are not politics.' Thus he exposed what he regarded as the fraudulent popular politics of his countrymen and revealed the focus of his own politics. Shaw joined the Fabian society in 1884 and he remained a Fabian educator all his life. The protagonists of his plays were more likely to be teachers than heroes and in public life he was more interested in delivering provocative critiques than in the politics of vote and policy. He was less enamoured of democracy than many socialists and there is evidence here, again, of the importance of the experience and perceptions of his early years. His fear of democracy as mobocracy is a Swiftian fear, for Shaw saw the real social divide as that between the civilized and barbaric elements of society, between the Houyhnhnms and Yahoos of *Gulliver's Travels*. 'I am a moral revolutionary', he declared, 'interested not in the class war, but in the struggle between human vitality and the artificial system of morality.' His primary target was not the class system itself, but middle-class morality, which, for all its stress on a self-help ethic and the other Victorian values of his youth, boiled down, he believed, to a single concern: 'Does it pay?'

It was a suspicion that this philosophy of profit was the only one which Shakespeare understood which led Shaw to wage his literary war on the bard. He always respected what he described as Shakespeare's unsurpassed command of 'word-music', but his literary heroes were artist-philosophers rather than word-musicians. Bunyan, Blake, Shelley, Ibsen, Morris and Nietzsche were the writers whose peculiar sense of the world he recognized as more or less akin to his own. He read Dickens and Shakespeare 'without shame or stint', but he regretted that their observations were never co-ordinated into a philosophy. Wagner and Mozart were, however, the most important influences of all, for music was so important to his development that he held that nobody could understand him without being 'soaked in symphonies and operas ... far more completely than in the literary drama'. He enjoyed the discipline and precision of music and equated the mastering of Wagner's operas with learning a philosophy.

For all this, there was a strong vein of self-parody running through Shaw. If he was Mephistopheles, he was also a self-confessed stage-villain. He declared that it was as Mr Punch that he had burst upon the literary scene and he acknowledged that he had the clown and the tragedian in him, and that the latter was always tripping up the former. Shaw enjoyed posing as the pedagogic Superman and courted publicity shamelessly, but he was never universally acclaimed. One recurrent complaint about him was that he was little better than a journalist, being too concerned with the bustle of the present to be a true artist. Yeats described him as the Joseph whose prosperity had brought his brother artists into the captivity of the press. Shaw retorted that journalism was the only true form of art, because the present was the only thing a man could hope to understand. Yeats could not accept this and saw Shaw as a man haunted by the mysteries he flouted; as 'an atheist who trembled in the haunted corridor'. This is a fair comment, for, although Shaw professed to believe in neither a transcendental God, nor in Art as God, he did once confess, in Yeatsian terms, that 'the power of Art' had, in his youth, been the only power 'religious enough' to save him from the spiritlessness of Irish Protestantism.

Shaw had a mixed critical reception in his later years. In 1956, the playwright John Whiting argued, in defence of the 'funny old man', that, in an age of timidity, it had been refreshing to have a writer who liked 'to hit things hard to see what happened'. This is exactly what Shaw did and, at his best, he made people think again about matters upon which they thought their opinions were decided. He also had the trick of being able to say outrageous, unpopular and cruel things in a way which left his audience uncertain when he was being sincere and when mischievous. 'Mark Twain and I are in very much the same position,' he confessed. 'We have to put things in such a way as to make people, who would otherwise hang us, believe that we are joking.' The challenge for the discerning reader is to navigate between the Shavian joke and the serious Shaw.

Editor's Note

Shaw's preferred spelling of Shakespeare as Shakespear and deliberate omission of inverted commas (e.g. dont for don't, youll for you'll) have been retained.

Shaw on Shaw

My speciality is being right when other people are wrong.

You Never Can Tell, Act IV, 1896

It was as Punch ... that I emerged from obscurity.

Preface to *Plays Unpleasant*, 1898

All autobiographies are lies. I do not mean unconscious, unintentional lies: I mean deliberate lies. No man is bad enough to tell the truth about himself during his lifetime.

'In the days of my youth', 1898

I have advertised myself so well that I find myself, whilst still in middle life, almost as legendary a person as the Flying Dutchman.

Preface to *Three Plays for Puritans*, 1900

I tell you that as long as I can conceive something better than myself I cannot be easy unless I am striving to bring it into existence or clearing the way for it. That is the law of my life.

Man and Superman, Act III, 1903

I dont believe in morality. I'm a disciple of Bernard Shaw.

The Doctor's Dilemma, Act III, 1906

The real secret of the cynicism and inhumanity of which shallower critics accuse me is the unexpectedness with which my characters behave like human beings, instead of conforming to the romantic logic of the stage.

Preface to *Mrs Warren's Profession*, 1907

I also am a journalist, proud of it, deliberately cutting out of my works all that is not journalism, convinced that nothing that is not journalism will live long as literature, or be of any use whilst it does live ... And so, let others cultivate what they call literature: journalism for me!

Preface to *The Sanity of Art*, 1907

I deal with all periods; but I never study any period but the present, which I have not yet mastered and never shall; and as a dramatist I have no clue to any historical or other personage save that part of him which is also myself ... The man who writes about himself and his own time is the only man who writes about all people and about all time.

Ib.

I have a professional reason for not drinking alcohol. The work I have to do depends for its quality on a very keen self-criticism. Anything that makes me easily pleased with myself instantly reduces the quality of my work.

The Review of Reviews, 1908

All Shaw's characters are himself: mere puppets stuck up to spout Shaw.

Fanny's First Play, Epilogue, 1911

I sing my own class: the Shabby Genteel, the poor Relations, the Gentlemen who are no Gentlemen.

Preface to *Immaturity*, 1921

I cannot deny that I have got the tragedian and I have got the clown in me; and the clown trips me up in the most dreadful way.

Address to the Royal Academy of Dramatic Art, 1928

I am of the true Shakespearian type: I understand everything and everybody, and am nobody and nothing.

Letter to Frank Harris, 20 June 1930

This book [Harris's projected biography of Shaw] is your chance of recovering your tall hat; and you want to throw it away for the sake of being in the fashion of O'Neill, Joyce, and George Moore. And even George does not imagine that force in literature is attained by calling a spade a f——g shovel. Even if it were, this sort of thing does not belong to your generation or mine, which should say all that it wanted to say without lessons from the forecastle and the barrack guard room.

Ib., 21 April 1931

I am a faith healer. You don't suppose I believe the bottles cure people? But the patient's faith in the bottle does.

Too True To Be Good, Act I, 1931

My father was an Irish Protestant gentleman of the downstart race of younger sons ... He had, however, been brought up to believe that there was an inborn virtue of gentility in all Shaws as partisans of William the Conqueror (the Dutch William of glorious, pious, and immortal memory, not the Norman adventurer).

Sixteen Self Sketches, 1949

I flatter myself that the unique survival of the Fabian Society among the forgotten wrecks of its rivals, all very contemptuous of it, was due not only to its policy, but in the early days to the one Irish element in its management.

Ib.

Happiness is never my aim ... I have neither time nor taste for such comas, attainable at the price of a pipeful of opium or a glass of whiskey.

Ib.

Shaw was full not only of Ibsen, but of Wagner, of Beethoven, of Goethe, and, curiously, of John Bunyan. The English way of being great by flashes: Shakespear's way, Ruskin's way, Chesterton's way ... could not disguise its incoherence from an Irishman ... His native pride in being Irish persists in spite of his whole adult career in England and his preference for English and Scottish friends.

Suggested to Frank Harris by Shaw, in *Ib.*

Human Life & Human Nature

[A pessimist:] A man who thinks everybody is as nasty as himself, and hates them for it.

The Unsocial Socialist, 1887

The people who get on in this world are the people who get up and look for the circumstances they want, and, if they can't find them, make them.

Mrs Warren's Profession, Act II, 1894

Immorality does not necessarily imply mischievous conduct: it implies conduct, mischievious or not, which does not conform to current ideals.

The Quintessence of Ibsenism, 1891

It is easy – terribly easy – to shake a man's faith in himself. To take advantage of that to break a man's spirit is the devil's work.

Candida, Act I, 1895

Do you think that the things people make fools of themselves about are any less real and true than the things they behave sensibly about?

Ib.

Self-sacrifice is the foundation of all nobility of character.

The Man of Destiny, 1895

Well, sir, you never can tell. That's a principle in life with me, sir. If youll excuse my having such a thing, sir.

You Never Can Tell, Act II, 1896

To ask him his intentions? What a violation of Twentieth Century principles!

Ib., Act III

All human progress involves, as its first condition, the willingness of the pioneer to make a fool of himself.

Cosmopolis, September 1896

The worst sin towards our fellow creatures is not to hate them, but to be indifferent to them: that's the essence of inhumanity.

The Devil's Disciple, Act II, 1897

That secret of heroism, never to let your life be shaped by fear of its end.

The Perfect Wagnerite, 1898

If human nature, which is the highest organization of life on this planet, is really degenerating, then human society will decay; and no panic-begotten penal measures can possibly save it: we must, like Prometheus, set to work to make new men instead of vainly torturing old ones.

Ib.

A man of great common sense and good taste – meaning thereby a man without originality or moral courage.

'Notes to *Caesar and Cleopatra*', 1898

When a stupid man is doing something he is ashamed of, he always declares that it is his duty.

Ib., Act III

Progress can do nothing but make the most of us all as we are.

'Epistle Dedicatory', *Man and Superman*, 1903

A lifetime of happiness! No man could bear it: it would be hell on earth.

Ib., Act I

We are ashamed of everything that is real about us; ashamed of ourselves, of our relatives, of our incomes, of our accents, of our opinions, of our experience, just as we are ashamed of our naked skins ... The more things a man is ashamed of, the more respectable he is.

Ib.

Nature is a pandar, Time a wrecker and Death a murderer.

Ib., Act III

There are two tragedies in life. One is to lose your heart's desire. The other is to gain it.

Ib., Act IV

Liberty means responsibility. That is why most men dread it.
'Maxims for Revolutionaries', *Ib.*

Men are wise in proportion, not to their experience, but to their capacity for experience.
Ib.

Make your cross your crutch; but, when you see another man do it, beware of him.
Ib.

Beware of the man who does not return your blow: he neither forgives you, nor allows you to forgive yourself.
Ib.

The man who listens to Reason is lost: Reason enslaves all whose minds are not strong enough to master her.
Ib.

Self-sacrifice enables us to sacrifice other people without blushing.
Ib.

A learned man is an idler who kills time with study.
Ib.

Self-denial is not a virtue: it is only the effect of prudence on rascality.
Ib.

Do not love your neighbour as yourself. If you are on good terms with yourself it is an impertinence; if on bad, an injury.
Ib.

Do not do unto others as you would that they should do unto you. Their tastes may not be the same.
Ib.

Except during the nine months before he draws his first breath, no man manages his affairs as well as a tree does.
Ib.

When a man wants to murder a tiger, he calls it sport; when the tiger wants to murder him, he calls it ferocity. The distinction between crime and justice is no greater.

Ib.

Life levels all men: death reveals the eminent.

Ib.

Live in contact with dreams and you will get something of their charm: live in contact with facts and you will get something of their brutality. I wish that I could find a country to live in where the facts were not brutal and the dreams not unreal.

John Bull's Other Island, Act I, 1904

What really flatters a man is that you think him worth flattering.

Ib., Act IV

There are only two qualities in the world: efficiency and inefficiency; and only two sorts of people: the efficient and the inefficient.

Ib.

Money is indeed the most important thing in the world; and all sound and successful personal and national morality should have this fact for its basis.

Preface to *The Irrational Knot*, 1905

The universal regard for money is the one hopeful fact in our civilization, the one sound spot in our social conscience. Money is the most important thing in the world. It represents health, strength, honour, generosity, and beauty as conspicuously as the want of it represents illness, weakness, disgrace, meanness, and ugliness.

Preface to *Major Barbara*, 1905

What a man is depends upon his character; but what he does, and what we think of what he does, depends on his circumstances.

Ib.

UNDERSHAFT: I took care … that you could be wasteful,
  careless, generous. That saved your soul from the seven
  deadly sins.
BARBARA: The seven deadly sins!
UNDERSHAFT: Yes, the deadly seven. Food, clothing, firing,
  rent, taxes, respectability and children. Nothing can lift
  those seven millstones from Man's neck but money; and the
  spirit cannot soar until the millstones are lifted.

Ib., Act II

Physically there is nothing to distinguish human society from
the farm-yard except that children are more troublesome and
costly than chickens and women are not so completely
enslaved as farm stock.

Preface to *Getting Married*, 1908

You dont learn to hold your own in the world by standing on
guard, but by attacking, and getting well-hammered yourself.

Ib.

It is immorality not morality that needs protection … for
morality with all the dead weight of human inertia and
superstition to hang on the back of the pioneer, and all the
malice of vulgarity and prejudice to threaten him, is
responsible for many persecutions and many martyrdoms.

The Shewing Up of Blanco Posnet, 1909

A life spent in making mistakes is not only more honourable
but more useful than a life spent doing nothing.

Preface to *The Doctor's Dilemma*, 1911

The truth is, hardly any of us have ethical energy enough for
more than one really inflexible point of honour.

Ib.

No man is scrupulous all round. He has, according to his
faculties and interests, certain points of honour, whilst in
matters that do not interest him he is careless and
unscrupulous.

Ib.

There is in man a specific lust for cruelty which infects even his passion for pity and makes it savage.

Ib.

Fashions, after all, are only induced epidemics.

Ib.

Use your health, even to the point of wearing it out. That is what it is for. Spend all you have before you die, and do not outlive yourself.

Ib.

The right to know is like the right to live. It is fundamental and unconditional in its assumption that knowledge, like life, is a desirable thing.

Ib.

Life does not cease to be funny when people die any more than it ceases to be serious when people laugh.

Ib., Act V

As long as I have a want, I have a reason for living. Satisfaction is deadly.

Overruled, 1912

What is life but a series of inspired follies? The difficulty is to find them to do.

Pygmalion, Act II, 1913

A man's interest in the world is only the overflow from his interest in himself.

Heartbreak House, Act III, 1919

When a prisoner sees the door of his dungeon open, he dashes for it without stopping to think where he shall get his dinner outside.

Preface to *Back to Methuselah*, 1920

Nature holds no brief for the human experiment: it must stand or fall by its results.

Ib.

It is courage, courage, courage that raises the blood of life to crimson splendour.

Ib., Part I.ii

It is long and hard and painful to create life: it is short and easy to steal the life others have made.

Ib.

Life is too short for men to take it seriously.

Ib., Part II

Life is a disease; and the only difference between one man and another is the stage of the disease at which he lives.

Ib.

It is the highest creatures who take the longest to mature, and are the most helpless during their immaturity.

Ib., Part III

Dancing is a very crude attempt to get into the rhythm of life.

Ib., Part V

The body always ends by being a bore. Nothing remains beautiful and interesting except thought, because the thought is the life.

Ib.

Humanity always fails me: Nature never.

Too True To Be Good, Act II, 1931

Naked bodies no longer shock us ... but the horror of the naked mind is still more than we can bear.

Ib., Act III

Z: I dont think the world is rightly arranged: do you?
A: We must take the world as we find it. It's we who are not rightly arranged.

Village Wooing, 1933

I loathe saving. It turns human nature sour.

Ib.

There are two sorts of people in the world: the people any one can live with and the people no one can live with.

The Millionairess, Act I, 1935

Oh, the deep end! the deep end! What is life if it is not lived at the deep end.

Ib.

Women, Love & Marriage

Women's dearest delight is to wound man's self-conceit, though man's deepest delight is to gratify hers. There is at least one creature lower than man.

An Unsocial Socialist, 1887

The fickleness of the women I love is only equalled by the infernal constancy of the women who love me.

The Philanderer, Act IV, 1893

The only way for a woman to provide for herself decently is for her to be good to some man that can afford to be good to her.

Mrs Warren's Profession, Act II, 1894

A man ought to be able to be fond of his wife without making a fool of himself about her.

Candida, Act I, 1895

I do not know whether women ever love. I rather doubt it: they pity a man, *mother* him, delight in making him love them; but I always suspect that their tenderness is deepened by their remorse for being unable to love him.

Letter to Ellen Terry, 6 April 1896

The ideal love affair is one conducted by post. My correspondence with Ellen Terry was a wholly satisfactory love affair ... She got tired of five husbands; but she never got tired of me.

Letter to Hesketh Pearson

The great advantage of a hotel is that it's a refuge from home life.

You Never Can Tell, Act II, 1896

Ask this man whom you have inspired and made brave, how many women have inspired him before; how many times he has laid the trap in which he has caught you; how often he has baited it with the same speeches; how much practice it has taken to make him perfect in his chosen part in life as the Duellist of Sex.

Ib., Act III

Remember: a man's power to love and admiration is like any other of his powers: he has to throw it away many times before he learns what is really worthy of it.

Ib.

Love cant give any man new gifts. It can only heighten the gifts he was born with.

Ib., Act IV

Women have to unlearn the false good manners of their slavery before they acquire the genuine good manners of their freedom.

Ib.

All matches are unwise. It's unwise to be born; it's unwise to be married; it's unwise to live; and it's wise to die.

Ib.

Love is assumed to be the only theme that touches all your audience infallibly ... And yet love is the one subject that the drawing room drama dare not present.

Preface to *Three Plays for Puritans*, 1900

I have a technical objection to making sexual infatuation a tragic theme. Experience proves that it is only effective in the comic spirit.

Ib.

A slave state is always ruled by those who can get round the masters: that is, by the more cunning of the slaves themselves ... The slavery of women is the tyranny of women. No fascinating woman ever wants to emancipate her sex: her object is to gather power into the hands of Man, because she knows she can govern him. She is no more jealous of his nominal supremacy than he himself is jealous of the strength and speed of his horse.

Letter to Clement Scott, January 1902

Women are supposed to have no political power; but clever
women put stupid husbands into parliament and into
ministerial offices quite easily.

Ib.

We laugh at the haughty American nation because it makes the
negro clean its boots and then proves the moral and physical
inferiority of the negro by the fact that he is a shoeblack; but
we ourselves throw the whole drudgery of creation on one sex,
and then imply that no female of any womanliness or delicacy
would initiate any effort in that direction. There are no limits to
male hypocrisy in this matter.

'Epistle Dedicatory', *Man and Superman*, 1903

It is the self-sacrificing women that sacrifice others most
recklessly.

Ib., Act I

Is the devil to have all the passions as well as all the good
tunes?

Ib.

Of all human struggles there is none so treacherous and
remorseless as that between the artist man and the mother
woman.

Ib.

You think that you are Ann's suitor; that you are the pursuer
and she the pursued; that it is your part to woo, to persuade, to
prevail, to overcome. Fool: it is you who are the pursued, the
marked down quarry, the destined prey.

Ib., Act II

It is a woman's business to get married as soon as possible, and
a man's to keep unmarried as long as he can.

Ib.

You can be as romantic as you please about love, Hector; but
you mustnt be romantic about money.

Ib.

What is virtue but the Trade Unionism of the married?

Ib., Act III

Marriage is a mantrap baited with simulated accomplishments and delusive idealizations.

Ib.

Those who talk most about the blessings of marriage ... are the very people who declare that if the chain were broken and the prisoners left free to choose, the whole social fabric would fly asunder. You cannot have the argument both ways. If the prisoner is happy, why lock him in?

Ib.

Beauty is all very well at first sight; but whoever looks at it when it has been in the house three days?

Ib., Act IV

Marriage is popular because it combines the maximum of temptation with the maximum of opportunity.

'Maxims for Revolutionists', *Ib.*

The best brought up children are those who have seen their parents as they are. Hypocrisy is not the parents' first duty.

Ib.

Home is the girl's prison and the woman's workhouse.

Ib.

The maternal instinct leads a woman to prefer a tenth share in a first rate man to the exclusive possession of a third rate one.

Ib.

There are two things that can be wrong with any man. One of them is a cheque. The other is a woman. Until you know that a man's sound on these two points, you know nothing about him.

The Doctor's Dilemma, Act II, 1906

Morality consists of suspecting other people of not being legally married.

Ib., Act III

There are couples who dislike each other furiously for several hours at a time; there are couples who dislike one another permanently; and there are couples who never dislike one another; but these last are people who are incapable of disliking anybody.

Preface to *Getting Married*, 1908

Home life as we understand it is no more natural to us than a
cage is natural to a cockatoo.

Ib.

The one point on which all women are in furious secret
rebellion against the existing law is the saddling of the right to
a child with the obligation to become the servant of a man.

Ib.

Marriage is tolerable enough in its way if youre easygoing and
dont expect too much from it. But it doesnt bear thinking about.

Getting Married, 1908

An English lady is not a slave to her appetite. That is what an
English gentleman seems incapable of understanding.

Ib.

Women upset everything. When you let them into your life,
you find that the woman is driving at one thing and youre
driving at another.

Pygmalion, Act II, 1913

I dont want to talk grammar. I want to talk like a lady.

Ib.

When our relatives are at home, we have to think of all their
good points or it would be impossible to endure them.

Heartbreak House, Act I, 1919

I am a woman of the world, Hector; and I can assure you that if
you will only take the trouble always to do the perfectly
correct thing, and to say the perfectly correct thing, you can do
just what you like.

Ib.

ELLIE: Why do women always want other women's husbands?
CAPTAIN SHOTOVER : Why do horse-thieves prefer a horse that
is broken in to one that is wild?

Ib., Act II

Women, having all the trouble and pain of creating human life,
are less tolerant of slaughterous waste of it.

Table Talk, 1924

No woman can shake off her mother. There should be no mothers: there should only be women, strong women able to stand by themselves, not clingers.

Too True to be Good, Act III, 1931

Well, sir, a man should have one woman to prevent him from thinking too much about women in general.

Ib.

Everyman thinks that every woman that steps into a railway carriage may be the right woman. But she is always a disappointment.

Village Wooing, 1933

The sex relation is not a personal relation. It can be irresistibly desired and rapturously consummated between persons who could not endure one another for a day in any other relation.

Letter to Frank Harris

Parentage is a very important profession, but no test of fitness for it is ever imposed in the interest of the children.

Everybody's Political What's What, 1944

Politics & War

The Fabian Society, having learned from experience that
Socialists cannot have their own way in everything any more
than other people, recognizes that in a Democratic community
compromise is a necessary condition of political progress.
Report of Fabian Policy: Tract 70, July 1891

The idealist is a more dangerous animal than a Philistine just
as a man is a more dangerous animal than a sheep.
The Quintessence of Ibsenism, 1891

We have no more right to consume happiness without
producing it than to consume wealth without producing it.
Candida, Act I, 1895

Social questions are produced by the conflict of human
institutions with human feeling.
The Humanitarian, May 1895

Mankind, being for the most part incapable of politics, accepts
vituperation as an easy and congenial substitute.
Notes to *The Devil's Disciple*, 1897

Idealism, which is only a flattering name for romance in
politics and morals, is as obnoxious to me as romance in ethics
and religion.
Preface to *Plays Pleasant*, 1898

If Despotism failed only for want of a capable benevolent
despot, what chance has democracy, which requires a whole
population of capable voters.
'Epistle Dedicatory', *Man and Superman*, 1903

Our political experiment of democracy, the last refuge of cheap
government.
Ib.

Tom Paine has triumphed over Edmund Burke and the swine
are now courted electors.
Ib.

The politician who once had to learn to flatter Kings has now to learn how to fascinate, amuse, coax, humbug, frighten, or otherwise strike the fancy of the electorate.

'The Revolutionist's Handbook', *Ib.*

Any person under the age of thirty, who, having any knowledge of the existing social order, is not a revolutionist, is an inferior. And yet revolutions have never lightened the burden of tyranny: they have only shifted it to another shoulder.

Ib.

The art of government is the organization of idolatry.

'Maxims for Revolutionists', *Ib.*

Democracy substitutes election by the incompetent many for appointment by the corrupt few.

Ib.

The reasonable man adapts himself to the world: the unreasonable one persists in trying to adapt the world to himself. Therefore all progress depends on the unreasonable man.

Ib.

He who slays a king and he who dies for him are alike idolators.

Ib.

Vulgarity in a king flatters the majority of the nation.

Ib.

Until a movement shows itself capable of spreading among brigands, it can never hope for a political majority.

Ib., Act III

Beware the pursuit of the Superman: it leads to an indiscriminate contempt for the human.

Ib.

He knows nothing and he thinks he knows everything. That points clearly to a political career.

Major Barbara, Act III, 1905

It is quite useless to declare that all men are born free if you deny that they are born good. Guarantee a man's goodness and his liberty will take care of itself.

Ib.

A healthy nation is as unconscious of its nationality as a healthy man of his bones. But if you break a nation's nationality it will think of nothing else but getting it back again.

Preface to *John Bull's Other Island*, 1906

A political scheme that cannot be carried out except by soldiers will not be a permanent one.

Ib.

Anarchism is a game at which the police can beat you.

Misalliance, 1910

Men are not governed by justice, but by law or persuasion. When they refuse to be governed by law or persuasion they have to be governed by force or fraud, or both.

Ib.

A King is an idol: that is why I am a Republican.

The New Age, 2 June 1910

Youll never have a quiet world till you knock the patriotism out of the human race.

O'Flaherty V.C., 1915

ERMYNTRUDE : What! You too worship before the statue of Liberty, like the Americans?
THE INCA : Not at all, Madam. The Americans do not worship the statue of Liberty. They have erected it in the proper place for a statue of Liberty: on its tomb.

The Inca of Perusalem, 1916

Revolutionary movements attract those who are not good enough for established institutions as well as those who are too good for them.

Preface to *Androcles and the Lion*, 1916

Neither the rulers nor the ruled understand high politics. They do not even know that there is such a branch of knowledge and political science; but between them they can coerce and enslave with the deadliest efficiency.

Preface to *Back to Methuselah*, 1920

Practical politicians are people who have mastered the art of using parliament to prevent anything being done.

Ib.

An election is a moral horror, as bad as a battle except for the blood: a mud bath for every soul concerned in it.

Ib., Part II

The worst cliques are those which consist of one man.

Ib., Part V

Any practical statesman will, under duress, swallow a dozen oaths to get his hand on the driving wheel.

Manchester Guardian, 27 December 1921

Democracy, as we practise it, is ruinous nonsense. All the republics are whited sepulchres.

Table Talk, 1924

Votes for Everybody and Votes for Anybody is making civilization a rush of Gadarene swine down a steep place into the sea.

Ib.

ARCHIBALD HENDERSON: You are a member of the Labour Party.
SHAW: Yes.
AH: Why?
SHAW: Why not? Would you have me support the idleness parties?

Ib.

Fascism is middle class Bolshevism; and Bolshevism ... is an emergency policy like martial law.

Ib.

Democracy always prefers second-bests.

Ib.

Trade Unionism is the capitalism of the working classes; its method is to get as much out of the employer and give him as little in return as possible ... Two centuries of capitalism have corrupted the wage worker as deeply as the employer.

Ib.

Idiots are always in favour of inequality of income (their only chance of eminence), and the really great in favour of equality.

The Intelligent Woman's Guide to Socialism and Communism, 1928

Moscow is built of English history written in London by Karl Marx.

The Apple Cart, Act II, 1929

The conflict is not really between royalty and democracy. It is between both and plutocracy, which, having destroyed the royal power by frank force under democratic pretexts, has bought and shallowed democracy. Money talks: money prints: money broadcasts: money reigns; and kings and labour leaders alike have to register its decrees, and even, by a staggering paradox, to finance its enterprises and guarantee its profits. Democracy is no longer bought: it is bilked.

Preface to *The Apple Cart*, 1930

Democracy ... is seldom more than a long word beginning with a capital letter, which we accept reverently or disparage contemptuously without asking any questions.

Ib.

The only man who had a proper understanding of Parliament was old Guy Fawkes.

On The Rocks, Act II, 1933

No country has ever been governed by the consent of the people, because the people object to being governed at all.

Ib.

Unless the highest court can be set in motion by the humblest individual, justice is a mockery.

Geneva, Act II, 1938

Man is a failure as a political animal. The creative forces which produce him must produce something better.

Ib., Act IV

A government which robs Peter to pay Paul can always depend on the support of Paul.

Everybody's Political What's What, 1944

I have lived to see modern Germany discard Hail, Mary! and substitute Heil, Hitler!; and for the life of me I cannot bring myself to regard the change as an improvement. It looks too like a revival of the worship of the ancient Egyptian god Ra, whose head was the head of a hawk.

Ib.

You can always tell an old soldier by the inside of his holsters and cartridge boxes. The young ones carry pistols and cartridges: the old ones, grub.

Arms and the Man, Act I, 1894

I never expect a soldier to think.

The Devil's Disciple, Act III, 1897

In the arts of life man invents nothing; but in the arts of death he outdoes Nature herself, and produces by chemistry and machinery all the slaughter of plague, pestilence and famine.

Man and Superman, Act III, 1903

In the arts of peace Man is a bungler.

Ib.

There is nothing in man's industrial machinery but his greed and sloth: his heart is in his weapons ... Man measures his strength by his destructiveness.

Ib.

You darent handle high explosives; but youre all ready to handle honesty and truth and justice and the whole duty of man, and kill one another at that game. What a country! What a world!

Major Barbara, Act III, 1905

Nothing is ever done in this world until men are prepared to kill one another if it is not done.

Ib., Act IV

All progress means war with Society.

Getting Married, 1908

Nations are like bees: they cannot kill except at the cost of their own lives.

Common Sense about the War, 1914

The British blockade won the war [in 1918]; but it is a wonder the British blockhead did not lose it. I suppose the enemy was no wiser. War is not a sharpener of wits.

Preface to *O'Flaherty V.C.*, 1919

War fever is a curious disease and very infectious.

Table Talk, 1924

We shall make wars because only under the strain of war are we capable of changing the world; but the changes our war will make will never be the changes we intended them to make.

The Simpleton of the Unexpected Isles, 1934

Mankind, though pugnacious, yet has an instinct which checks it on the brink of self-destruction.

Preface to *Geneva,* 1938

Class

The test of a man or woman's breeding is how they behave in a quarrel.

The Philanderer, Act III, 1893

There are three sorts of people in the world: the low people, the middle people, and the high people. The low people and the high people are alike in one thing: they have no scruples, no morality. The low are beneath morality, the high above it ... It is the middle people who are dangerous: they have both knowledge and purpose. But they, too, have their weak point. They are full of scruples: chained hand and foot by their morality and respectability.

The Man of Destiny, 1895

The man with toothache thinks everyone happy whose teeth are sound. The poverty stricken man makes the same mistake about the rich man.

'Maxims for Revolutionists', *Man and Superman*, 1903

Ladies and gentlemen are permitted to have friends in the kennel, but not in the kitchen.

Ib.

Gambling promises the poor what property performs for the rich: that is why the bishops dare not denounce it fundamentally.

Ib.

Titles distinguish the mediocre, embarrass the superior, and are disgraced by the inferior.

Ib.

A moderately honest man with a moderately faithful wife, moderate drinkers both, in a moderately healthy house: that is the true middle-class unit.

Ib.

We must be thoroughly democratic, and patronize everybody without distinction of class.

John Bull's Other Island, Act IV, 1904

In the middle classes, where the segregation of the artificially limited family in its little brick box is horribly complete, bad manners, ugly dresses, awkwardness, cowardice, peevishness and all the petty vices of unsociability flourish like mushrooms in a cellar.

Preface to *Getting Married*, 1908

Independence? That's middle class blasphemy. We are all dependent on one another, every soul of us on earth.

Pygmalion, Act V, 1913

I have to live for others and not for myself; that's middle class morality.

Ib.

The man who cannot see that starvation, overwork, dirt, and disease are as anti-social as prostitution – that they are the vices and crimes of a nation, and not merely its misfortunes – is (to put it as politely as possible) a hopelessly Private Person.

Preface to *Mrs Warren's Profession*, 1902

MENDOZA : I am a brigand, I live by robbing the rich.
TANNER : I am a gentleman: I live by robbing the poor.

Man and Superman, Act III, 1903

In an ugly and unhappy world the richest man can purchase nothing but ugliness and unhappiness.

'Maxims for Revolutionists', *Ib.*

Security, the chief pretence of civilization, cannot exist where the worst of dangers, the danger of poverty, hangs over everyone's head.

Preface to *Major Barbara*, 1905

The greatest of evils and the worst of crimes is poverty ... our first duty – a duty to which every other consideration should be sacrificed – is not to be poor.

Ib.

CUSINS : Do you call poverty a crime?
UNDERSHAFT: The worst of all crimes. All the other crimes are
   virtues beside it.   *Ib.*, Act IV

As to snobbishness, ignorant men are always snobbish, because Nature abhors a vacuum.

The Clerk, February 1908

LORD SUMMERHAYS: Reading is a very dangerous amusement, Tarleton. I wish I could persuade some of your free library people of that.
TARLETON: Why, man, it's the beginning of education.
SUMMERHAYS: On the contrary, it's the end of it. How can you dare teach a man to read until you have taught him everything else first?

Misalliance, 1910

PICKERING: Have you no morals, man?
DOOLITTLE: Can't afford them, Governor.

Pygmalion, Act II, 1913

Undeserving poverty is my line. Taking one station in society with another, it's – it's – well, it's the only one that has any ginger to it, to my taste.

Ib.

I'm one of the undeserving poor: that's what I am. Think of what that means to a man. It means that he's up agen middle-class morality all the time ... What is middle-class morality? Just an excuse for not giving me anything.

Ib.

When I meet a man who makes a hundred thousand a year, I take off my hat to that man ... and call him brother.

Heartbreak House, Act I, 1919

England & Ireland

It is all work and no play in the brain department that makes John Bull such an uncommonly dull boy.

Music in London, 1890-94

The English are a race apart. No Englishman is too low to have scruples: no Englishman is high enough to be free of their tyranny. But every Englishman is born with a certain miraculous power that makes him master of the world. When he wants a thing, he never tells himself that he wants it. He waits patiently until there comes into his mind, no one knows how, a burning conviction that it is his moral and religious duty to conquer those who possess the thing he wants. Then he becomes irresistible. Like the aristocrat, he does what he pleases and grabs what he covets: like the shopkeeper, he pursues his purpose with the industry and steadfastness that come from strong religious conviction and [a] deep sense of moral responsibility. He is never at a loss for an effective moral attitude. As the great champion of freedom and national independence, he conquers and annexes half the world, and calls it Colonization. When he wants a new market for his adulterated Manchester goods, he sends a missionary to teach the natives the Gospel of Peace. The natives kill the missionary; he flies to arms in defence of Christianity; fights for it; conquers for it; and takes the market as a reward from heaven. In defence of his island shores, he puts a chaplain aboard his ship; nails a flag with a cross on it to his top-gallant mast; and sails to the ends of the earth, sinking, burning, and destroying all who dispute the empire of the seas with him. He boasts that a slave is free the moment his foot touches British soil; and he sells the children of his poor at six years of age to work under the lash in his factories for sixteen hours a day.

The Man of Destiny, 1895

There is nothing so bad or so good that you will not find an Englishman doing it; but you will never find an Englishman in the wrong. He does everything on principle. He fights you on patriotic principles; he robs you on business principles; he enslaves you on imperial principles; he bullies you on manly principles; he supports his king on loyal principles and cuts off his king's head on republican principles ... His watchword is Duty; and he never forgets that the nation which lets its duty get on the opposite side to its interest is lost.

Ib.

We dont bother much about dress and manners in England, because, as a nation, we dont dress well and weve no manners.

You Never Can Tell, Act I, 1896

If you lived in London, where the whole system is one of false good-fellowship, and you may know a man for twenty years without finding out that he hates you like poison, you would soon have your eyes opened. There we do unkind things in a kind way: we say bitter things in a sweet voice: we always give our friends chloroform when we tear them to pieces.

Ib.

A dwarf – a creature with energy enough to make himself strong of body and fierce of passion, but with a brutish narrowness of intelligence and selfishness of imagination: too stupid to see that his own welfare can only be compassed as part of the welfare of the world, too full of brute force not to grab vigorously at his own gain. Such dwarfs are quite common in London.

The Perfect Wagnerite, 1898

This is Britannus, my secretary. He is an islander from the western end of the world, a day's voyage from Gaul ... He is a barbarian, and thinks that the customs of his tribe and island are the laws of nature.

Caesar and Cleopatra, Act II, 1898

It seems impossible to root out of an Englishman's mind the notion that vice is delightful, and that abstention from it is privation.

Preface to *Mrs Warren's Profession*, 1902

I will not allow you or any man to treat me as if I were a mere member of the British public. I detest its prejudices; I scorn its narrowness; I demand the right to think for myself.

Man and Superman, Act I, 1903

Your pious English habit of regarding the world as a moral gymnasium built expressly to strengthen your character.

Ib.

Very nice sort of place, Oxford, I should think, for people that like that sort of place.

Ib., Act II

Englishmen never will be slaves: they are free to do whatever the Government and public opinion allow them to do.

Ib., Act III

An Englishman thinks he is moral when he is only uncomfortable.

Ib.

Englishmen ... always lean sincerely to virtue's side, as long as it costs them nothing either in money or in thought. They feel deeply the injustice of foreigners who allow them no credit for this conditional high-mindedness.

'The Revolutionist's Handbook', *Ib.*

Englishmen hate Liberty and Equality too much to understand them. But every Englishman loves a pedigree.

Ib.

When we learn to sing that Britons never will be masters we shall make an end of slavery.

'Maxims for Revolutionists', *Ib.*

An Irishman's heart is nothing but his imagination.

John Bull's Other Island, Act I, 1904

Standing here between you the Englishman, so clever in your foolishness, and the Irishman, so foolish in your cleverness, I cannot in my ignorance be sure which of you is the more deeply damned.

Ib., Act IV

The English are extremely particular in selecting their butlers, whilst they do not select their barons at all, taking them as the accident of birth sends them. The consequences include much ironic comedy.

The Irrational Knot, 1905

In good society in England ... men drivel at all ages by repeating silly formulas with an air of wisdom. Schoolboys make their own formulas out of slang ... When they reach your age, and get political private secretaryships, and things of that sort, they drop slang and get their formulas out of *The Spectator* and *The Times*.

Major Barbara, Act III, 1905

Every true Englishman detests the English. We are the wickedest nation on earth; and our success is a moral horror.

Ib.

An Englishman never asks what he is doing or why he is doing it. He prefers not to know, as he suspects that whatever it is, it is something wrong. The Scotchman, nurtured on the Shorter Catechism, is able to use his brains, and, therefore, likes using them. The Irishman, on the other hand, knows what he is doing without any study of the subject whatever. The result is that he often gets there before the reflective Scotchman or the recalcitrant Englishman.

Clare Market Review, January 1906

When power and riches are thrown haphazard into children's cradles as they are in England, you get a governing class without industry, character, courage, or real experience; and under such circumstances reforms are produced only by catastrophes followed by panics in which 'something must be done'. Thus it costs a cholera epidemic to achieve a Public Health Act, a Crimean War to reform the Civil Service, and a gunpowder plot to disestablish the Irish Church. It was by the light, not of reason, but of the moon, that the need for paying serious attention to the Irish land question was seen in England.

Preface to *John Bull's Other Island*, 1906

The insensibility of the English governing classes to philosophical, moral and social considerations ... is tempered, as we Irish well know, by an absurd susceptibility to intimidation.

Ib.

Even if Home Rule were as unhealthy as an Englishman's
eating, as intemperate as his drinking, as filthy as his smoking,
as licentious as his domesticity, as corrupt as his commerce, as
cruel as his prisons, and as merciless as his streets, Ireland's
claim to self-government would still be as good as England's.
Ib.

The English have no respect for their language, and will not
teach their children to speak it ... It is impossible for an
Englishman to open his mouth without making some other
Englishman hate or despise him.
Preface to *Pygmalion*, 1913

We are a nation of governesses.
New Statesman, 12 April 1913

The British officer seldom likes Irish soldiers; but he always
tries to have a certain proportion of them in his battalion ...
because even the most cowardly Irishman feels obliged to
outdo an Englishman in bravery.
Preface to *O'Flaherty V.C.*, 1919

Go anywhere in England where there are natural, wholesome,
contented, and really nice English people, and what do you
always find? That the stables are the real centre of the
household ... There are only two classes in good society in
England: the equestrian classes and the neurotic classes.
Heartbreak House, Act III, 1919

Talk to an Englishman about anything serious, and he listens
to you curiously for a moment just as he listens to a chap
playing classical music. Then he goes back to his marine golf,
or motoring, or flying, or women, just like a bit of stretched
elastic when you let it go.
Back to Methuselah, Part III, 1920

I am a tolerably good European in the Nietzschean sense, but a
very bad Irishman in the Sinn Fein or Chosen People sense.
Preface to *Immaturity*, 1921

We were not fairly beaten, my lord. No Englishman is ever
fairly beaten.   *Saint Joan*, Scene iv, 1923

How can what an Englishman believes in be heresy? It is a contradiction in terms.

Ib.

Scratch an Englishman and find a Protestant.

Ib.

Nationalism must now be added to the refuse pile of superstitions. We are now citizens of the world; and the man who divides the race into elect Irishmen and reprobate foreign devils (especially Englishmen) had better live on the Blaskets where he can admire himself without much disturbance.

Irish Statesman, 15 September 1925

As to Coercion Acts, the worst English one on record is a perfect Magna Charter compared with the one imposed by the Free State ... The little finger of the Free State is thicker than the loins of the Castle; but the Irish stand it because it is their own government.

Ib.

What Englishman will give his mind to politics as long as he can afford to keep a motor car?

The Apple Cart, Act I, 1929

Breakages, Ltd, the biggest industrial corporation in the country.

Ib.

God help England if she had no Scots to think for her.

Ib., Act II

When you find some country gentleman keeping up the old English customs at Christmas and so forth, who is he? An American who has just bought the place.

Ib.

An English crowd will never do anything mischievous or the reverse, while it is listening to speeches. And the fellow who makes the speeches can be depended on never to do anything else.

On The Rocks, Act I, 1933

Give me English birds and English trees, English dogs and
Irish horses, English rivers and English ships; but English men!
No, No, No!

In Good King Charles's Golden Days, 1939

Eternal is the fact that the human creature born in Ireland and
brought up in its air is Irish.

'Ireland Eternal and External', 1948

I believe Ireland, as far as the Protestant gentry is concerned, to
be the most irreligious country in the world. I was Christened
by my uncle; and as my godfather was intoxicated and did not
turn up, the sexton was ordered to promise and vow in his
place, precisely as my uncle might have ordered him to put
more coals on the fire ... Of the seriousness with which English
families took this rite I had no conception; for Irish
Protestantism was not then a religion: it was a side in political
faction, a class prejudice, a conviction that Roman Catholics are
socially inferior persons who will go to Hell when they die and
leave Heaven in the exclusive possession of Protestant ladies
and gentlemen.

Sixteen Self Sketches, 1949

Art & Culture

The great artist is he who goes beyond the demand, and, by supplying works of a higher beauty and a higher interest than have yet been perceived, succeeds, after a brief struggle with its strangeness, in adding this fresh extension of sense to the heritage of the race.

The Sanity of Art, 1895

To understand a saint, you must hear the devil's advocate; and the same is true of the artist.

Ib.

The artist's rule must be Cromwell's: 'Not what they want, but what is good for them.' This rule, carried out in a kindly and sociable way, is the secret to success in the long run at the theatre as elsewhere.

The Saturday Review, 20 April 1895

The material of the dramatist is always some conflict of human feeling with circumstances.

The Humanitarian, May 1895

All art is gratuitous; and the will to produce it, like the will to live, must be held to justify itself.

The Saturday Review, 2 April 1898

I am convinced that fine art is the subtlest, the most seductive, the most effective means of moral propagandism in the world, excepting only the example of personal conduct.

Preface to *Mrs Warren's Profession*, 1902

What we call education and culture is for the most part nothing but the substitution of reading for experience, of literature for life, of the obsolete fictitious for the contemporary real.

'Epistle Dedicatory', *Man and Superman*, 1903

The true artist will let his wife starve, his children go barefoot, his mother drudge for his living at seventy, sooner than work at anything but his art. To women he is half vivisector, half vampire.

Ib., Act I

Like all poets I have a passion for pugilism.

How He Lied To Her Husband, 1904

Nobody can say a word against Greek: it stamps a man at once as an educated gentleman.

Major Barbara, Act I, 1905

I believe in Michael Angelo, Velasquez, and Rembrandt; in the might of design, the mystery of colour, the redemption of all things by Beauty everlasting, and the message of Art that has made these hands blessed.

The Doctor's Dilemma, Act IV, 1906

'Art for art's sake' means in practice 'Success for money's sake'. Great art is never produced for its own sake. It is too difficult to be worth the effort.

Preface to *Three Plays by Brieux*, 1910

You dont expect I know what to say about a play when I dont know who the author is, do you? ... If it's by a good author, it's a good play, naturally. That stands to reason.

Fanny's First Play, Epilogue, 1911

Assassination is the extreme form of censorship.

The Rejected Statement, *The Shewing Up of Blanco Posnet*, 1917

The art of the dramatic poet knows no patriotism.

Preface to *Heartbreak House*, 1919

You use a glass mirror to see your face: you use works of art to see your soul.

Back to Methuselah, Part V, 1920

Without art the crudeness of reality would make the world unbearable.

Ib.

I avoid plots like the plague. I have warned young playwrights again and again that a plot is like a jigsaw puzzle, enthralling to the man who is putting it together, but maddeningly dull to the looker on.

Table Talk, 1924

You cannot combine the pursuit of money and the pursuit of art.

Ib.

All great Art and Literature is propaganda.

Preface to *On the Rocks*, 1933

Plot has always been the curse of serious drama, and indeed of serious literature of any kind. It is so out of place that Shakespear never could invent one.

Foreword to *Cymbeline Refinished*, 1937

When I am writing a play I never invent a plot: I let the play write itself and shape itself, which it always does even when up to the last moment I do not foresee the way out.

Postscript to *Back to Methuselah*, 1944

What power did I find in Ireland religious enough to redeem me from this abomination of desolation [the Church of Ireland]? Quite simply, the power of Art.

Sixteen Self Sketches, 1949

A drama critic is a man who leaves no turn unstoned.

The New York Times, 5 November 1950

The quality of a play is the quality of its ideas.

The New Statesman, 1950

[Upon declining to sell Samuel Goldwyn the screen rights to his work:] The trouble, Mr Goldwyn, is that you are only interested in art and I am only interested in money.

Music & Musicians

If I do not care to rhapsodize much about Mozart, it is because I am so violently prepossessed in his favour that I am capable of supplying any possible deficiency in his work by my imagination ... In my small boyhood I by good luck had an opportunity of learning the Don thoroughly; and if it were only for the sense of the value of fine workmanship which I gained from it, I should still esteem that lesson the most important part of my education.

The World, 9 December 1891

[On Brahms:] The Leviathan Maunderer ... His requiem is patiently borne only by the corpse.

The Star, 1892

Grieg's *Peer Gynt* music ... consists of two or three catchpenny phrases served up with plenty of orchestral sugar.

The World, 1892

Brahms is just like Tennyson, an extraordinary musician, with the brains of a third rate village policeman.

Letter to Packenham Beatty, 4 April 1893

All my musical self-respect is based on my keen appreciation of Mozart's work. It is still as true as it was before the Eroica symphony existed, that there is nothing better in art than Mozart's best.

Music in London, 1890-94

In the ardent regions where all the rest are excited and vehement, Mozart alone is completely self-possessed: where they are clutching their bars with a grip of iron and forging them with Cyclopean blows, his gentleness of touch never deserts him: he is considerate, economical, practical under the same pressure of inspiration that throws your Titan into convulsions. That is the secret of his unpopularity with Titan fanciers. With Mozart you are safe from inebriety. Hurry, excitement, eagerness, loss of consideration, are to him purely comic or vicious states of mind.

Ib.

The fact is, there are no rules, and there never were any rules, and there never will be any rules of musical composition except rules of thumb; and thumbs vary in length, like ears.

Ib.

Music will express any emotion, base or lofty. She is absolutely unmoral.

Ib.

I am highly susceptible to the force of all truly religious music, no matter to what Church it belongs; but the music of my own church ... is to be found in *Die Zauberflöte* and the ninth symphony.

Ib.

The pianoforte is the most important of all musical instruments: its invention was to music what printing was to poetry.

The Fortnightly Review, 1894

To master Wagner's music dramas is to learn a philosophy.
The Humanitarian, 1895

Beethoven was the first man who used music with absolute integrity as the expression of his own emotional life. Others had shown how it could be done ... but Beethoven made this, and nothing else, his business.

The Saturday Review, 14 November 1896

Wagner did not begin a movement: he consummated it. He was at the summit of the nineteenth century school of dramatic music ... And those who attempt to carry on his Bayreuth traditions will assuredly share the fate of the forgotten purveyors of second-hand Mozart a hundred years ago.

The Perfect Wagnerite, 1898

To enjoy *Tristan* it is only necessary to have had one serious love affair; and though the number of persons possessing this qualification is popularly exaggerated, yet there are enough to keep the work alive.

Ib.

Hell is full of musical amateurs: music is the brandy of the damned.

Man and Superman, Act III, 1903

Edward Elgar, the figure head of music in England, is a composer whose rank it is neither prudent nor indeed possible to determine. Either it is one so high that only time and posterity can confer it, or else he is one of the seven Humbugs of Christendom.

Music and Letters, 1920

You can rave about Stravinsky without the slightest risk of being classed a lunatic by the next generation.

Ib.

When Satan makes impure verses, Allah sends a divine tune to cleanse them.

The Adventures of the Black Girl in her Search for God, 1932

Music was so important in my development, that nobody can really understand my art without being soaked in symphonies and operas, in Mozart, Verdi and Meyerbeer, to say nothing of Handel, Beethoven and Wagner, far more completely than in the literary drama and its poets and playwrights.

Letter to St.John Ervine

Religion & Science

'Original sin' is the will doing mischief. 'Divine grace' is the will doing good.

The Quintessence of Ibsenism, 1891

Like all highly developed literatures, the Bible contains a great deal of sensational fiction, imagined with intense vividness, appealing to the most susceptible passions, and narrated with a force which the ordinary man is quite unable to resist.

The Saturday Review, 27 November 1897

There is only one religion, though there are a hundred versions of it.

Preface to *Plays Pleasant,* 1898

Every genuine religious person is a heretic and therefore a revolutionist.

'The Revolutionist's Handbook', *Man and Superman,* 1903

Beware of the man whose god is in the skies.

'Maxims for Revolutionists', *Ib.*

The savage bows down to idols of wood and stone: the civilized man to idols of flesh and blood.

Ib.

If you go to Heaven without being naturally qualified for it, you will not enjoy yourself there.

Ib., Act III

Hell is the home of honour, duty, justice, and the rest of the seven deadly virtues.

Ib.

I am somewhat surprised to hear a member of your [Roman] Church quote so essentially a Protestant document as the Bible.

John Bull's Other Island, Act IV, 1904

Sir: when you speak to me of English and Irish you forget that I am a Catholic. My country is not Ireland nor England, but the whole mighty realm of my Church. For me there are but two countries: heaven and hell, but two conditions of men: salvation and damnation.

Ib.

I am a Millionaire. That is my religion.

Major Barbara, Act II, 1905

I am a sort of collector of religions; and the curious thing is that I find I can believe in them all.

Ib.

I cant talk religion to a man with bodily hunger in his eyes.

Ib.

Science is always simple and always profound. It is only the half-truths that are dangerous.

The Doctor's Dilemma, Act I, 1906

There is at bottom only one genuinely scientific treatment for all diseases, and that is to stimulate the phagocytes.

Ib.

Martyrdom is the only way in which a man can become famous without ability.

Preface to *Fabian Essays,* 1908

What God hath joined together no man shall ever put asunder: God will take care of that.

Getting Married, 1908

I took the broad path because I was a man and not a snivelling canting turning-the-other-cheek apprentice angel serving his time in a vale of tears. They talked Christianity to us on Sundays; but when they really meant business they told us never to take a blow without giving it back, and to get dollars.

The Shewing Up of Blanco Posnet, 1909

Heaven, as conventionally conceived, is a place so inane, so dull, so useless, so miserable, that nobody has ever ventured to describe a whole day in heaven, though plenty of people have described a day at the seaside.

Preface to *Misalliance*, 1910

Children must be taught some sort of religion. Secular education is an impossibility. Secular education comes to this: the only reason for ceasing to do evil and learning to do well is that if you do not you will be caned. This is worse than being taught in a church school that if you become a dissenter you will go to hell; for hell is presented as the instrument of something eternal, divine and inevitable; you cannot evade it the moment the schoolmaster's back is turned.

Ib.

Ive got a soul: dont tell me I havnt. Cut me up and you cant find it. Cut up a steam engine and you cant find the steam. But, by George, it makes the engine go.

Misalliance, 1910

LORD SUMMERHAYS: Do you not pray as common people do?
LINA: Common people do not pray, my lord: they only beg.

Ib.

John the Baptist may have been a Keir Hardie; but Jesus of Matthew is of the Ruskin-Morris class.

Preface to *Androcles and the Lion*, 1916

The conversion of a savage to Christianity is the conversion of Christianity to savagery.

Ib.

When Jesus called Peter from his boat, he spoiled an honest fisherman, and made nothing better out of the wreck than a salvation monger.

Ib.

Whether you think Jesus was God or not, you must admit that he was a first class political economist.

Ib.

All great truths begin as blasphemies.

Annajanska, 1917

God's trustiest lieutenants often lack official credentials. They may be professed atheists who are also men of honour and high public spirit.

Preface to *Back to Methuselah,* 1920

Every genuine scientist must be a metaphysician.

Ib.

Without their fictions, the truths of religion would for the multitude be neither intelligible nor even apprehensible; and the prophets would prophesy and the teachers teach in vain.

Ib.

Well, as the serpent used to say, why not?

Ib.

He who bears the brand of Cain shall rule the earth.

Ib.

I have the utmost respect for the magnificent discoveries which we owe to science. But any fool can make a discovery. Every baby has to discover more in the first years of its life than Roger Bacon ever discovered in his laboratory.

Ib.

The Lord's Prayer I used once or twice as a protective spell.

Preface to *Immaturity,* 1921

The churches must learn humility as well as teach it.

Preface to *Saint Joan,* 1923

If ever I utter an oath again may my soul be blasted to eternal damnation!

Ib., scene ii

The Jews generally give value. They make you pay, but they deliver the goods. In my experience the men who want something for nothing are invariably Christians.

Ib., scene iv

The Crusader comes back more than half a Saracen.

Ib.

Must then a Christ perish in torment in every age to save those that have no imagination?

Ib., Epilogue

'Many people who have found God have not liked him [said the old gentleman] and have spent the rest of their lives running away from him. Why do you suppose you would like him?'

'I don't know' said the black girl, 'But the missionary has a line of poetry that says that we needs must love the highest when we see it.'

'That poet was a fool,' said the old gentleman. 'We hate it; we crucify it; we poison it with hemlock; we chain it to a stake and burn it alive.'

The Adventures of the Black Girl in her Search for God, 1932

These fellows who run after God crying 'Oh, that I knew where I might find Him', must have a tremendous opinion of themselves to think that they could stand before him.

Ib.

My first doubt as to whether God could really be a good Protestant was suggested by the fact that the best voices available for combination with my mother's in the works of the great composers had been unaccountably vouchsafed to Roman Catholics.

Sixteen Self Sketches, 1949

Shakespeare & Other Writers

The fact is that we are growing out of Shakespear ... His characters still live; his word pictures of woodland and wayside still give us a Bank-holiday breath of country air ... but we have nothing to hope from him, and nothing to learn from him – not even how to write plays, though he does that so much better than most modern dramatists.

The Saturday Review, 11 July 1896

In playing Shakespear, play to the lines, *through* the lines, *on* the lines, but never *between* the lines. There simply isn't time for it ... Nothing short of a procession or a fight should make anything so extraordinary as a silence during a Shakespearian performance.

Letter to Ellen Terry, 23 September 1896

Even when Shakespear, in his efforts to be a social philosopher, does rise for an instant to the level of a sixth rate Kingsley, his solemn self-complacency infuriates me. And yet, so wonderful is his art, that it is not easy to disentangle what is unbearable from what is irresistible.

The Saturday Review, 5 December 1896

My capers are part of a bigger design than you think: Shakespear, for instance, is to me one of the Towers of the Bastille, and down he must come.

Letter to Ellen Terry, 27 January 1897

The Englishman, slave to every sentimental ideal and dupe of every sensuous art, will have it that his great national poet is a thinker. The Frenchman, enslaved and duped only by systems and calculations, insists on his hero being a sentimentalist and artist. That is why Shakespear is esteemed a master-mind in England, and wondered at as a clumsy barbarian in France.

The Saturday Review, 26 February 1898

It does not follow ... that the right to criticize Shakespear involves the power of writing better plays. And in fact ... I do not profess to write better plays.

Preface to *Three Plays for Puritans*, 1900

The author of Everyman was no mere artist, but an artist-philosopher, and ... the artist-philosophers are the only sort of artists I take quite seriously ... Plato and Boswell, as the dramatists who invented Socrates and Dr Johnson, impress me more than the romantic playwrights ... Bunyan, Blake, Hogarth, and Turner (these four apart and above all the English classics), Goethe, Shelley, Schopenhauer, Wagner, Ibsen, Morris, Tolstoy and Nietzsche are among the writers whose peculiar sense of the world I recognize as more or less akin to my own ... I read Dickens and Shakespear without shame or stint; but their pregnant observations and demonstrations of life are not co-ordinated into any philosophy or religion: on the contrary, Dickens's sentimental assumptions are violently contradicted by his observations; and all that you miss in Shakespear you find in Bunyan, to whom the true heroic came quite obviously and naturally.

'Epistle Dedicatory', *Man and Superman*, 1903

Put your Shakespearian hero and coward, Henry V and Pistol or Parolles, beside [Bunyan's] Mr Valiant and Mr Fearing, and you have a sudden revelation of the abyss that lies between the fashionable author who could see nothing in the world but personal aims and the tragedy of their disappointment or the comedy of their incongruity, and the field preacher who achieved virtue and courage by identifying himself with the purpose of the world as he understood it.

Ib.

Shakespear's power lies in his enormous command of word-music, which gives fascination to his most blackguardly repartees and sublimity to his hollowest platitudes ... Shakespear's weakness lies in his complete deficiency in that highest sphere of thought, in which poetry embraces religion, philosophy, morality ... His characters have no religion, no politics, no conscience, no hope, no convictions of any sort ... His test of the worth of life is the vulgar hedonist test ... like most middle-class Englishmen, bred in private houses, he was a very incompetent thinker, and took it for granted that all inquiry into life began and ended with the question 'Does it pay?'

The Daily News, 27 April 1905

With the single exception of Homer, there is no eminent writer, not even Sir Walter Scott, whom I can despise so entirely as I despise Shakespear when I measure my mind against his ... It would positively be a relief to me to dig him up and throw stones at him.

Dramatic Opinions and Essays, II, 1907

The reason why Shakespear and Molière are always well spoken of and recommended to the young is that their quarrel is really a quarrel with God for not making men better. If they had quarrelled with a specified class of persons with incomes of four figures for not doing their work better, or for doing no work at all, they would be denounced as seditious, impious, and profligate corrupters of morality.

Preface to *Three Plays by Brieux*, 1909

This in all actuarial probability is my last play and the climax of my eminence, such as it is.

Preface to *Shakes versus Shav*, 1949

SHAV: ... Peace, jealous Bard:
    We both are mortal. For a moment suffer
    My glimmering light to shine.
        [A light appears between them]
SHAKES : Out, out brief candle!
        [He puffs it out. Darkness. The play ends.]
Shakes versus Shav, 1949

Charles Dickens, whose books, though classed as novels and duly hampered with absurd plots which nobody ever remembers, are really extraordinarily vivid parables. All the political futility which has forced men of the calibre of Mussolini, Kemal, and Hitler to assume dictatorship might have been saved if people had only believed what Dickens told them in *Little Dorrit*.

Introduction to *Collected Prefaces*, 1938

Byron was as little a philosopher as Peter the Great: both were instances of that rare and useful, but unedifying variation, an energetic genius born without the prejudices and superstitions of his contemporaries.

'Epistle Dedicatory', *Man and Superman*, 1903

I have not wasted my life trifling with literary fools as Johnson did when he should have been shaking England with the thunder of his spirit.

Preface to *Misalliance*, 1910

Don Quixote, Brand, and Peer Gynt are, all three, men of action seeking to realize their ideals in deeds ... Their castles in the air are more beautiful than castles of brick and mortar; but one cannot live in them.

The Quintessence of Ibsenism, 1891

Ibsen never presents his play to you as a romance for your entertainment: he says, in effect, 'Here is yourself and myself, our society, our civilization. The evil and the good, the horror and the hope of it, are woven out of your life and mine.'

The Saturday Review, 27 April 1895

Oscar Wilde is to me our only thorough playwright. He plays with everything: with wit, with philosophy, with drama, with actors and audience, with the whole theatre. Such a feat scandalizes the Englishman, who can no more play with wit and philosophy than he can with a football or a cricket bat.

The Saturday Review, 12 January 1895

Wells and I, contemplating the Chesterbelloc, recognize at once a very amusing panto elephant, the front legs being the very exceptional and unEnglish individual Hilaire Belloc, and the hind legs that extravagant freak of French nature, G.K. Chesterton.

New Age, 15 February 1908

In Ireland they try to make a cat cleanly by rubbing its nose in its own filth. Mr Joyce has tried the same treatment on the human subject. I hope it may prove successful.

Letter to Slyvia Beach, 11 June 1921

When they asked me to pay three guineas for *Ulysses* I said I
would not go a penny above seven and sixpence ... I could not
write the words Mr Joyce used: my prudish hand would refuse
to form the letters and I can find no interest in his infantile
clinical incontinences, or in the flatulations which he thinks
worth mentioning ... *Ulysses* is a document, the outcome of a
passion for documentation that is as fundamental as the artistic
passion ... Joyce is driven by his documentary *daimon* to place
on record the working of a young man's imagination for a
single day in the environs of Dublin ... The Dublin 'jackeens' of
my day ... were very like that. Their conversation was dirty;
and it defiled their sexuality ... You cannot carry out moral
sanitation any more than physical sanitation, without indecent
exposures. Get rid of the ribaldry that Joyce describes and
dramatises, and you get rid of *Ulysses* ... Suppress the book
and have the ribaldry unexposed; and you are protecting dirt
instead of protecting morals. If a man holds up a mirror to
your nature and shows you that it needs washing – it is no use
breaking the mirror. Go for soap and water.

Table Talk, 1924

Mark Twain and I are in very much the same position. We
have to put things in such a way as to make people, who
would otherwise hang us, believe that we are joking.

Ib.

Stray Sayings & Attributions

I'm only a beer teetotaller, not a champagne teetotaller.

Candida, Act III, 1895

SWINDON : What will History say?
BURGOYNE : History, sir, will tell lies as usual.

The Devil's Disciple, Act III, 1897

THEODOTUS : Without history, death will lay you beside your meanest soldier.
CAESAR : Death will do that in any case. I ask no better grave.
THEODOTUS : Will you destroy the past?
CAESAR : Ay, and build the future with its ruins.

Caesar and Cleopatra, Act II, 1898

He who has never hoped can never despair.

Ib., Act IV

The novelties of one generation are only the resuscitated fashions of the generation before last.

Preface to *Three Plays for Puritans*, 1900

Effectiveness of assertion is the alpha and omega of style.

'Epistle Dedicatory', *Man and Superman*, 1903

The philanthropist is a parasite on misery.

Ib., Act I

The only Golden Rule is that there are no golden rules.

'Maxims for Revolutionists', *Ib.*

Youth, which is forgiven everything, forgives itself nothing: age, which forgives itself everything, is forgiven nothing.

Ib.

The most intolerable pain is produced by prolonging the keenest pleasure.

Ib.

He who can, does. He who cannot, teaches.

Ib.

Decency is Indecency's conspiracy of silence.

Ib.

Take care to get what you like or you will be forced to like what you get.

Ib.

Hatred is the coward's revenge for being intimidated.
Major Barbara, Act III, 1905

Let no one suppose that the words doctor and patient can disguise from the parties the fact that they are employer and employee.
Preface to *The Doctor's Dilemma*, 1906

All professions are conspiracies against the laity.
Ib., Act I

It's just as unpleasant to get more than you bargain for as to get less.
Getting Married, 1908

Optimistic lies have such immense therapeutic value that a doctor who cannot tell them convincingly has mistaken his profession.
Preface to *Misalliance*, 1910

It's all the young can do for the old, to shock them and keep them up to date.
Fanny's First Play, 'Induction', 1911

Make me a beautiful word for doing things tomorrow, for that surely is a great and blessed invention.
Back to Methuselah, Part I, 1920

Silence is the most perfect expression of scorn.

Ib., Part V

Examinations are useless: they test knowledge, not capacity.

Table Talk, 1924

LORD NORTHCLIFFE: The trouble with you, Shaw, is that you
   look as if you were the famine in the land.
SHAW: The trouble with you, Northcliffe, is that you
   look as if you were the cause of it.

[Dancing is] a perpendicular expression of a horizontal desire.

Quoted in *New Statesman*, 23 March 1962

If all economists were laid end to end, they would not reach a
conclusion.

[Reply to a lady who wrote that as he had the best mind in the
world and she the best body, they would produce the perfect
child:] But what if the child inherited my body and your
brains?

[Shaw's response to the solitary hiss heard during the applause
at the curtain call of *Arms and the Man*, 1894:] I quite agree
with you, sir, but what can two do against so many?

[Replying to a hostess's enquiry as to whether he was enjoying
himself at her party:] Certainly, there is nothing else here to
enjoy.

England and America are two countries divided by a common
language.

SHAW: Would you sleep with me for £1,000?
Lady: I would consider the proposal.
SHAW: Would you sleep with me for £1?
Lady: What do you think I am ?
SHAW: Madam, we have established what you are. We are
   simply haggling over the price.